A Wisl

Hedg
Scieens

MICHAEL POLLOCK

Cassell

The Royal Horticultural Society

THE ROYAL HORTICULTURAL SOCIETY

Cassell Educational Limited
Villiers House, 41/47 Strand
London WC2N 5JE
for the Royal Horticultural Society

First published 1994

British Library Cataloguing in Publication Data
A catalogue record for this book is available from the British Library

ISBN 0-304-32036-6

Photographs by Photos Horticultural (pp. 1, 13, 16, 53); Michael Pollock (pp. 7, 8, 10, 20, 23, 24, 26, 29, 31, 32, 33, 34, 37, 41, 42, 44, 45, 50, 58, 61, 62, 63); Harry Smith Collection (pp. 4, 38, 46, 47, 49, 51, 55, 56, 57)
Line drawings by Mike Shoebridge

Phototypesetting by RGM Associates, Southport
Printed in Hong Kong by Wing King Tong Co. Ltd

Cover: Hedges may take many forms. Box, *Buxus sempervirens*, is an ideal low edging for ingeniously shaped knots and parterres, while beech (*Fagus* spp.) – in purple and green – grows tall to give privacy and shelter.
p.1: Wall-like yew hedges at Knightshayes Court, Devon.
   Photographs by Photos Horticultural
Back cover: Yew, *Taxus baccata*, can be trimmed into smooth decorative shapes and wall-like hedges. Although often thought of as slow growing, with time it grows large.
   Photograph by Michael Pollock

Contents

Why Make a Hedge?

Hedges have an important place in gardening and their planting, maintenance, renovation and, indeed, removal pose many questions. A little study of principles and practical experience is worthwhile because hedge and screen making is an expensive investment in time and purchases; and the result of one's decision making will usually be prominent and long lasting.

Think of a hedge as a continuous row of closely planted trees or shrubs, kept to a height of no more than 15 ft (4.5 m) but usually around 6 ft (1.8 m). Taller rows, suitable for very large gardens, estates and farmland, are better known as belts. Shrubby plantings of less than 18 in. (45 cm) height, often seen bordering pathways or incorporated in very formal garden designs, are usually referred to as edging. All these forms are grown to serve one or a number of purposes.

A screen is really any vertical narrow structure established to decorate, mask or protect. It may comprise a wall or fence constructed of stone, wood or even plastic, or living plants trained as a hedge or belt. Most hedges are effectively screens though of course not all screens are hedges.

The term 'fedge' is sometimes used to describe intermediate structures where fence or trellis screens are combined with climbers and other plants, for example, clematis and bamboo. These often feature in examples of Japanese interpretative garden design, and deserve wider use.

The most common reason for planting a hedge is to define the area limits of a garden, and for most people a row of living plants is more pleasing than fabricated fencing.

Hedges and screens give privacy by removing or reducing the distraction of some neighbouring sights and activities, and thereby create a sense of isolation or transport from the actual surroundings. Well made and maintained boundary hedges provide a secure barrier. In many instances, including those where the need is to prevent children and pets from straying out, it may be sufficient to have only a single-line hedge or screen. Other situations need more determined effort like chain-link fencing with

Yew (*Taxus baccata*), with its fine-textured foliage, is ideal for clipping into topiary shapes

5

hedge plants established close by to obscure it. The best security hedge is one made from spiny plants such as berberis, hawthorn (*Crataegus*), blackthorn (*Prunus spinosa*) and holly (*Ilex*), all of which are trimmable. Where security is important around large gardens, and some expense is possible, it is a good plan to allow such plants to grow untrimmed against a boundary line and to plant more attractive shrubs or conifers in front of the thorny barrier.

Trained to suitable height, hedges give welcome shade in summer, and protection from cold winds in winter. Hedges and screens may be planned to divide a garden into sections; a very effective means of suggesting increased size of plot. Planting boundary and internal hedges makes a real contribution to attractive garden design by defining particular theme areas, the most obvious being spring, summer and winter plant collections; or perhaps sub-gardens of herbs, scented plants or a water feature. Used in this way hedges introduce an element of surprise into the garden layout. The visual impact of shrubberies and especially herbaceous borders is much enhanced where a trimmed hedge provides a sympathetic backdrop.

There are many situations where a hedge serves as an attractive garden feature of itself by reason of flower, foliage or berry production. Clipped and trained hedges can be used skilfully to extend the line of buildings and lessen their stark effect or to provide a topiary feature.

A hedge or screen will obscure an unattractive view. There may be vistas spoilt by distant urban or industrial development, nearby buildings which blight or are out of keeping with the surroundings; and, within the garden, storage and clothes-drying areas or compost and rubbish heaps. Well-developed hedges give an added dimension of interest in a garden as a means for bird roosting and nesting, besides shelter and accommodation for other small animals and insects.

FOR NOISY SITUATIONS

Dense evergreen hedges have some useful effect in reducing noise level from nearby railways and roads. Conifers are the best choice for this purpose and should be maintained with a minimum of trimming. The degree of noise suppression is directly influenced by the density of the established barrier, and for most benefit plantings must be at least two rows deep. The effectiveness of hedges for noise reduction is variable in practice depending not only on density of foliage but on plant age and maintenance

The hedge-demonstration area at the RHS Garden, Wisley, Surrey

standards, and particularly on the relative elevation of the noise source and the garden. Evergreen hedges are more likely to deaden rather than eliminate noise altogether. Analysis of air quality in gardens adjoining busy roads suggests that levels of chemical pollutant are unlikely to be of harmful significance with regard to contamination of edible crops, but dense hedging will of course reduce free movement of such air where the situation is of concern.

MICROCLIMATE

All hedges produce a garden microclimate different to the growing environment outside the protected area. From the gardener's point of view, most of the influences are beneficial but there are some counter-balancing disadvantages. The well-protected garden site is likely to be subjected to shade, and whereas this can be beneficial in facilitating an ideal growing climate for certain ornamental plants, it can be an enormous disadvantage for fruit and especially vegetable growing. Here it is sensible to consider deciduous subjects which permit some light penetration during winter while still providing effective shelter. Enhanced soil and air temperature within the developed microclimate benefits seed germination, early growth and maturity, and winter survival but may also encourage the harbouring of birds, small animals and insects which become garden pests. Similarly, restricted air flow provides a more favourable climate for the development of disease pathogens. Plants growing in the lee of an established hedge usually receive less natural rainfall by reason of its deflection over the 'shadow' area. Natural water availability will be reduced anyway for a variable width each side of an established hedge due to competing root activity.

The smaller the garden the greater are most of the disadvantages associated with microclimates; and they are of course additional to considerations of cost and maintenance time – and all such factors must be thought through.

WIND SHELTER

Apart from any other reason there is an overwhelming case for planting hedges to provide shelter from wind.

The most obvious effects of wind are physical damage to

An evergreen shelter belt, dramatically shaped by wind action, growing on an exposed coastal site

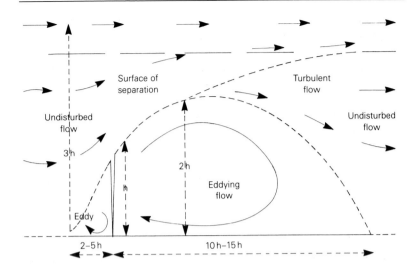

Diagrammatic representation of air movement around a near-solid cross-wind barrier

buildings and structures, plant breakage, the weakening of root anchorage and 'scorching' of leaves. In situations of extreme exposure there may be soil erosion, shoot and leaf damage from salt deposit or sand blow, and dramatic stunting of plant growth. Less obvious but most important to the gardener is water and heat loss from plants and the soil due to increased transpiration and evaporation. These effects slow down plant establishment and growth besides possibly hindering cultivations, spraying and irrigation. Windy conditions in the garden reduce the activity of pollinating insects in summer, and increase heat loss from green-houses in winter. There is experimental evidence of the highly beneficial effects of shelter on plant growth and all gardeners should give high priority to this consideration.

Shelter can be provided by fabricated screens or living barriers and the aim should always be to maintain a permeable profile in order to filter rather than totally obstruct the wind flow. Wind striking a solid or near-solid barrier is deflected upwards and over the obstruction, creating an area of low pressure to leeward. Resulting suction draws down air currents which give rise to intense turbulence causing more damage than the original wind. Theoretically ideal is a permeable hedge or other barrier of 60% solid:40% porosity. Deciduous species best suit this requirement, but there is a fair degree of licence in practice because even apparently very dense hedges open up in windy conditions.

Planning

Planning a hedge line requires understanding of the principles described together with knowledge or guidance on plant suitability. Careful forethought is essential to keep down the costs of maintenance, or even removal where a hedge eventually proves unsuitable or overbearing. The ultimate height and spread of boundary hedges must be envisaged. Will they give rise to excessive shading? Will they obstruct overhead service lines? Will they overhang and be a potential hazard to roadways? How are they to be contained to avoid such problems, and at what likely cost?

There is great scope for disputes with neighbours, or even legal action, over hedge encroachment and boundaries so it is sensible to discuss planting intentions at the outset, and agree the necessary arrangements for clipping or pruning on both sides of the hedge or screen. Thought might also be given to the potential loss of vista from a neighbour's property.

Especially in small gardens, where hedges may of necessity be planted close to buildings, consider also the likely invasion of roots into drains or foundations. Moisture-loving plants such as willow and poplar are notorious culprits to be avoided, but as a general rule gross hedge or screen specimens should not be allowed to develop in the confines of a small garden.

For seclusion and security it may be necessary to make a continuous hedge around the plot perimeter and in this case a variety of plants looks best.

Planning for the special advantage of wind protection raises important questions. The direction of prevailing wind in the British Isles is from the south-west but cold north-easterly winds are often particularly troublesome. Directional intensity varies with locality and the effects of wind are greatly influenced by the lie of surrounding land. There may be natural shelter from land mass or woodland, exposure to wind funnelling in valleys or gales off the sea. Local reconnaissance and observation by no more than looking at a wind vane on windy days, and noting the apparent effects of wind on plant growth, are good starting points where planning from scratch.

An archway through a hedge of mature yew (*Taxus baccata*) with, on the left, a topiary feature being trained on a frame

LAYOUT

As a principle in all hedge layout, it is helpful to understand that reduction of wind speed occurs over a distance of up to 30 times hedge height to leeward. At this limit the wind velocity is usually approximately the same as where unobstructed to windward of the hedge; and the closer a point is to the hedge line on the leeward side the more effective the shelter. For practical purposes effective windbreak influence is generally accepted to extend to a distance of 10 times the hedge or screen height to leeward. A hedge trained to grow to a manageable height of 8½ ft (2.5 m) will provide useful wind protection over a distance of 85 ft (25 m), at which point the next line should be planted. On sites of extreme exposure such as hilltops or right on the coast this distance should be halved. The velocity of deflected windstream is reduced up to a height of approximately one and a half times the height of the barrier (see p. 9). Where possible a hedge or screen should extend well beyond the width of the area or feature to be protected because there will be potentially damaging turbulence at the edges.

The course of surface wind is influenced by land contour, and accelerates along the line of a natural valley. In such situations a hedge should ideally be orientated at right angles to the channelled flow; and it will be increasingly ineffective at an angle less than 45° to the direction of the wind.

The provision of hedges and screens for wind protection on sloping ground is challenging. The natural lie of the land will usually cause the wind flow to be directed upwards so that the lower parts of a slope are relatively unaffected. Planting hedges and screens principally as windbreaks at the bottom of a slope therefore makes little or no contribution towards protecting land higher up. In some situations hedge planting across a slope at its lower levels obstructs air drainage and as cold air backs up the hillside frost damage is accentuated. Hedge planting at the top of a windward-facing slope is justified where a garden is situated on a flattened ridge, but where the site falls away from a ridge there will be minimal benefit. In some orientations the long shadows formed, especially during short days, will restrict the growth of plants. Gardens sloping face on to the wind are most effectively sheltered by planting across the slope at a mid point. On less directly exposed sites hedge lines should be planted with the slope.

Low hedges of lavender (*Lavandula angustifolia*) and box (*Buxus sempervirens* 'Suffruticosa') edging formal gravel paths

Any gap in a hedge causes accelerated wind flow, and in exposed localities it is quite common for component plants to be blown down as a result of increased air pressure at these points; and losses may be progressive along the row with succeeding gales. Wherever possible plant a wind baffle in front of or beyond an access point to reduce the velocity of funnelled wind. Careful plant thinning along a hedge line each side of a substantial gap achieves the same purpose. Questions frequently arise on the siting of hedges and screens near to greenhouses, and much depends on the size of the garden. In order to minimize structural damage and heat and light loss, the hedge or screen should be maintained to a height not less than that of a point half way between the ridge and gutter of the greenhouse, and sited no closer than four times its maximum height from the structure. A light-permeable profile is desirable especially in winter months.

PROSPECTING THE SITE

Hedge and screen making is an expensive undertaking so there must be thorough care in site selection. Location will often be dictated by one or more preset conditions or requirements, but in all cases the best possible choice must be made so that there will be strong root development for firm plant anchorage and effective extraction of soil moisture and nutrients.

Soil depth and drainage are first considerations, and if the site is not well known both should be assessed by digging sample holes to two-spade depth along the proposed planting line. If a compacted layer is encountered it should be examined for thickness, and the site only used if the 'pan' can be readily broken up during full preparation to allow root penetration and drainage. Only a few woody plants, such as willows, poplars and alders naturally thrive in wet soil conditions, and all newly-planted stock is vulnerable to waterlogging.

PREPARATIONS FOR PLANTING

The easiest planting site is one already under good cultivation where young hedge and screen plants can establish with a minimum of competition. Almost as straightforward is the site covered with well-maintained mown grass sward where turf can be incorporated to spade depth.

The greatest challenge is on sites where perennial weeds such as couch grass, docks, ground elder and brambles must be cleared along the hedge line, for they will otherwise restrict early development by competition, and in many cases be a perpetual unsightly nuisance. Non-persistent weedkillers are useful but to justify cost and effort these must be used, strictly according to the product instructions, during the season of active growth. Most effective is the often daunting expedient of regular systematic forking out, best done during summer months when hot, dry weather assists in desiccation. To clear severe infestation of perennial weeds planned effort is necessary over more than one season ahead of planting. On large garden sites frequent cultivation with a rotary digger can be done, again during summer months, but there will be damage to soil structure and the site must be carefully hand worked subsequently to remove regenerating root portions.

A month or two ahead of planting mark out the hedge or screen line and dig a strip 3 ft (90 cm) wide. The easiest way is to take out a spade-deep trench 1 ft (30 cm) wide across the width of the strip and transport the soil to the far end of the strip and pile it nearby. If the preliminary inspection showed evidence of a compacted layer below spade depth it is important to break this up with a fork. Where the planting is being made into a mown grass sward, skim off the turf to 2 in. (5 cm) depth in strips about 1 ft × 1 ft (30 cm × 30 cm), invert into the bottom of the small prepared trench and chop it up. Then dig the soil beneath the skimmed area inverting it into the trench to bury the chopped turf. When planting into grass sward it is easiest to cultivate a continuous planting strip as described; but where the hedge or screen plants are to be set out at 6 ft (1.8 m) stations or more apart individual planting places can be prepared. An arable strip can be dealt with in exactly the same way, any surface weed growth being turned in to the dug trench. Digging progresses by preparing a new trench continually along the marked out planting strip, and on reaching the end the soil transported from the first trench is used to fill in the last one.

Planting

MANURES AND FERTILIZERS

Different views exist on the benefits of incorporating organic matter into the planting site. Where plants are set out in well-dressed soil it is likely that early roots will be less inclined to explore at depth, with the possible consequence of weak anchorage. On the other hand planting into a soil devoid of organic matter means that moisture is less effectively retained, and lack of water in the soil at establishment time can be just as detrimental as waterlogging. Where garden soil is known to be reasonably fertile with good water-holding properties there is no need to import organic matter. Otherwise, and especially on sandy sites, it is sensible practice to incorporate to spade depth animal or plant waste which is at least 12 months old.

On established garden sites restrict supplementary fertilizers to dressings likely to maintain nutrient fertility, such as an application of no more than 4 oz per sq yd (136 g per sq m) of Growmore (7:7:7). Old pastureland will possibly be low in phosphate which can disadvantage hedge and screen plant establishment, and highly acid soil means interference with nutrient uptake in the case of many candidate plants. These special circumstances should be dealt with by additionally dressing with superphosphate and lime. Applications of straight nitrogen should not be given at planting time as they will be at most harmful and at least a waste of money.

Supplementary fertilizer dressings are best forked in to 6 in. (15 cm) depth as a second light cultivation just before planting.

WHEN AND WHAT TO PLANT

Planting in October or November allows early regrowth of roots in the following spring. This is the best course except in very exposed situations, especially on hilltops or very near to the sea, where winter gales often disturb or damage plants. Spring planting is the alternative but the later start in root production means that plants

Beech hedges (*Fagus sylvatica*) can hold their copper-coloured autumn foliage throughout winter

17

will be more vulnerable in dry periods of early summer. Planting into frozen or even temporarily waterlogged ground must not be done.

Plants are available either growing in containers or as bare-root plants lifted from the nursery. Container-grown plants, which are on offer all the year round, are much more costly than bare-rooted ones, and planting them out in summer is risky practice.

As a general rule the younger the plants are when set out the better, because the growth check is less and good root structure is developed *in situ*. Small plants are cheaper than large ones because they have been in the nurseryman's care for a shorter period. There are situations where the benefit of larger specimens in providing quick cover is quite justified, and with very special care such plants well grown in containers will establish better than large specimens of nursery-dug plants.

Container-raised plants must be critically inspected at the time of purchase. Top growth should be sturdy and in healthy condition. Most important, there must be good root development and this can only be ascertained by inverting the plant so that the container may be temporarily removed. An ideal condition is where the roots are evidently healthy and can be seen to have explored all areas of the pot without having been there so long as to become pot bound. Plants will not otherwise develop strong root systems in the permanent site. It is equally important to check that stock is not too recently potted, clearly demonstrated where on removal of the container little root exploration is seen and the compost readily falls apart. Thoroughly water plants in containers prior to planting. Bare-root plants lifted in the dormant season should be chosen for sturdy root systems not excessively pruned or damaged at lifting. If received when planting cannot be carried out immediately the bundles should be opened and the plants temporarily 'heeled in' to a trench and covered with moist soil. If received late when the outside ground is frozen it is best to temporarily store bundles intact under cover. It is good practice to soak the roots of lifted plants for a short while prior to permanent planting or 'heeling in'

PLANTING METHOD

For most of the hedge and screen purposes considered one line of plants is enough. In a garden precise positioning of the component plants is hardly critical and making the individual measured planting stations against a taut line set down the middle of the prepared site will suffice.

Setting a marker board across a site line where precise plant positioning is desirable. The central cane and the marker board are subsequently removed and the planting hole prepared

Plant set in the hole and roots loosely covered with soil. The marker board is then replaced in order to check planting position and depth. With the board removed, soil is gently firmed around the plant

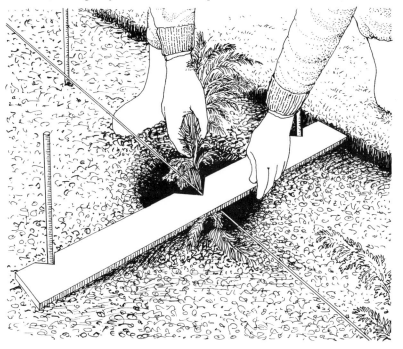

A tree shelter belt principally comprising fast-growing Italian alder, *Alnus cordata*

Where greater accuracy is preferred a marker board can be used, which has the extra advantage of helping gauge a consistent depth of planting at each station. The board is made of a narrow strip of wood as shown on p. 19, and the central notch is engaged around a cane marking the exact planting station. Additional canes are inserted at each of the smaller notches, and the marker board and central cane removed. The planting hole is then prepared, and the board fixed back around the two retained canes. The plant can then be exactly positioned, to a correct depth, against the central notch.

Planting holes must be large enough to accommodate existing roots without restriction or pruning, and at least as deep as the rootball or planting level in the nursery.

Remove containers of any sort before planting, and gently tease apart the root systems at the base only. Gently shake bare-root plants up and down as the removed soil is returned to the planting hole, to aid infilling. Gentle, even treading firms the plant, and if the soil is dry each planting place should be well watered.

Planting distances vary with purpose and species, and may well be influenced by the cost of plants. The period for a hedge to become thick and effective is of course affected by the closeness of planting. Stations of 2–3 ft (60–90 cm) are quite suitable for a very wide range of subjects including *Escallonia*, yew and cypress, providing early cover and mutual anchorage. Choice plants may be set out more widely,whilst cheaper subjects such as hawthorn and privet, and dwarf hedges or edging such as lavender and box, are suitably planted at distances down to 10 in. (25 cm) apart.

It is not good practice to stake plants established for hedging purposes because strong roots develop best where the plant can naturally flex in the wind. However, in situations of extreme exposure as on some hilltops or close to the sea it will be necessary to provide support and this is best done by soft tying to a continuous horizontal fence wire – which must be regularly inspected to avoid friction damage or stem constriction.

CARE AFTER PLANTING

In some gardens young plants will have to be protected from rabbit damage. Individual plant guards are appropriate for well-spaced choice subjects, otherwise a correctly buried mesh wire fence or even a proprietary electric one will be required.

Where a hedge or screen is being established on a site of extreme wind exposure, thought should be given to providing a temporary low artificial screen to windward. This could also combine as a rabbit-proofing measure. In some cases, especially where choice species are to be grown to a good height, nurse cover can be provided with cheaper, faster-growing plants of more robust habit. Any sort of barrier will protect the establishing hedge or living screen from the worst physical damage and loosening, and reduce transpiration from the plants and evaporation from the soil.

It is essential that young hedge and screen transplants have sufficient water during the early establishment period. The need is critical in spring and early summer, and water should be applied as a thorough drenching evenly and lightly by hose, watering can, or best of all from a low-level drip line where there are adequate water supplies. Half-hearted sprinkling of the soil surface is not only quite ineffective but wasteful of water and time.

Plants put out in a dry spring will benefit from daily damping over of aerial parts, best done during the evening.

Weathered organic matter incorporated prior to planting aids water retention, and its use as a surface mulch applied to a depth of 2–3 in. (5–7.5 cm) immediately after planting greatly slows water evaporation. Mulching material should only be applied to soil which is thoroughly moist, and there must be periodic inspection beneath the mulch to assess the need for watering.

Rotted animal manure or garden compost makes a suitable mulching material. Bark and wood chip products are good alternatives although they are liable to unsightly scattering after wind or bird foraging. Wood derivatives especially can deplete the soil of nitrogen as they decompose but this is only significant where incorporated rather than used as a surface mulch. Black polythene sheet, applied as continuous strips or as individual 'spats' around plants provides an equally effective means of moisture conservation and is a suitable choice where organic matter is not available; but it is unsightly and requires special care in securing. Where no mulching is carried out there must be even greater watchfulness for watering need.

Weeds in hedge or screen rows mean competition for moisture and nutrients, and it is always worth the effort of removing them at a very early stage of development because where neglected the job becomes more difficult and daunting. The importance of clearing weeds before planting has already been emphasized and where there are signs of re-establishment annual and perennial sorts must be removed quickly and carefully.

All of the mulching treatments discussed are equally valuable in suppressing annual weed growth, where applied to a depth of at least 2 in. (5 cm) on weed-free ground. If a ground mulch cannot be used, and regular cultivation is not possible, recourse may be made to recommended residual weedkillers applied at very low doses; but in the situation of young establishing plants this is the least agreeable of the three options.

In comparative studies mulched trees and shrubs have consistently performed better than unmulched ones, making significantly faster early growth and becoming more firmly established.

ROUTINE CARE

The foregoing advice on aftercare concentrates on the importance of attention during the early stages of hedge establishment. Mature hedges and screens are unlikely to need continuing protection from rabbit damage, and by reason of their deep root systems they

A mature hedge of hornbeam (*Carpinus betulus*) photographed as autumn approaches. The dead leaves are retained throughout winter

are usually capable of extracting adequate water from the soil at depth. However, in prolonged periods of drought on shallow or sandy soils not naturally retentive of moisture it is possible for well-established hedges and screens to suffer. Most deciduous subjects will tolerate and recover from such stress even if there is some leaf fall, but in evergreens, and conifers especially, arrested growth may be followed by progressive dying of foliage and branches from ground level. A serious consequence of the unsightly browning is that there is invariably no regrowth and in the long term the hedge remains bare at its base. Such conditions should be prepared for as it is quite possible to have even a mature hedge disfigured in this way. It is not usually practicable to undertake thorough watering of well-established hedge rows, especially when the need is likely to arise at a time of water shortage, but on vulnerable sites the risk can be much reduced by continuing the use of generous organic mulching beyond the early establishment phase.

Pruning and Trimming

PRUNING AFTER PLANTING

Whatever the purpose in providing a high hedge or screen there is need to encourage early growth, with well-furnished branches right down to ground level. For formal hedges and screens plants such as privet, hawthorn, blackthorn and tamarisk should be cut back to within 10 cm (4 in.) of ground level immediately after planting. Conifers, hollies, yew, laurel and most other evergreens should not be cut at all at this time. Beech, hornbeam and most deciduous species will benefit from light trimming, reducing the overall size by no more than one third, but from spring planting this treatment is best withheld until the following autumn. Informal hedge and screen plants should be left unpruned until well established.

SHAPING AND TRIMMING

Hedge trimming is laborious, but it can give great satisfaction. A well-kept formal hedge or screen complements the best of gardens and flatters other sorts, making a conspicuous contribution to small gardens as well as large ones. There are important reasons for trimming besides the obvious effect of visual impact. Hedges and screens require containment to avoid reaching unmanageable heights or overshadowing other plants, obstructing vistas, overhead services or pathways. Untrimmed hedges of most subjects will sooner or later become straggly and unsightly, and where shelter is required the effectiveness will be lost. Timely trimming encourages a replenishment of flower and fruit-bearing shoots, especially in informal hedge and screen species; and it is an opportunity to remove dead, damaged or old wood.

As discussed, there are different purposes for and types of hedges and screens and in all cases the approach to trimming needs to be considered at the planning stage. There are hardly any instances where it is not an essential operation. Formal hedges and screens

A skilfully maintained yew hedge profile (*Taxus baccata*), with gently sloping sides

are characterized by their line and neatness, and privet and yew are perhaps the best-known examples from small suburban and large rural gardens respectively. Once established they require trimming at least once a year with shears or powered cutters. Informal hedges are usually more appropriate to gardens where there is sufficient space to accommodate a reasonable amount of natural spread, and plants such as camellia and hydrangea are representative. Here annual trimming to varying severity is usually though not always necessary; and it is carried out with secateurs, so that the term 'pruning' is really more appropriate.

As will be seen, there are very many examples of plants which are chosen for formal and informal hedging, for example berberis and cotoneaster; and there are quite acceptable intermediate stages of formality and informality in how plants may be trained to make a striking contribution to the garden scene.

Whether a planting is intended as a formal or informal feature the same trimming practice may be adopted in the year following planting. The few species cut hard back to ground level at planting time should have about half of the subsequent season's growth removed. This will encourage branching and early development of a broad framework. Those plants shortened by about one third at

A hedge of *Lonicera nitida* benefits from a sloping top and regular clipping in order to keep the growth dense and contained

planting time – which probably represents the largest group of hedge and screen plants – should have the pruning treatment repeated after a full season's growth, with all side shoots lightly trimmed. Conifers and other evergreen subjects should again be left uncut except for minimal shortening of untidy side shoots and the possible complete removal of those very badly placed. The aim with this last group must be to keep a single leader shoot in growth right up to the required hedge or screen height.

Given good site preparation, stock choice, early after care and satisfactory weather conditions, plants may be expected to establish steadily over the season following planting. Even in the best of all conditions the rate of growth will vary greatly according to the chosen plant species. Box and holly are examples of the slowest growing evergreens, the larger-leafed escallonias and the Leyland cypress the fastest: most evergreen and deciduous plants come variously in between. So it is wise to get to know your chosen plants from other gardens or at least by reference to authoritative books.

FORMAL TRAINING

Formal hedges need most careful training in the establishment years, with the fixed objective of ensuring that the width at the top is never greater than the width at the bottom. Hedges and screens with a 'top heavy' section profile are unattractive and become more so year by year. More important, there is a natural shading of lower growths which leads to bare sections as the hedge or screen ages. Furthermore, there is a much greater risk of the weight of snow pulling the hedge apart in its early years, and although an occasional likelihood such damage can be devastating and irreparable.

The most usual advice is to make a hedge of narrow width with sloping sides and a flat top. It is certainly a good choice to have tapering sides but most gardeners will find it easier to maintain vertical ones. Jigs or frames specially made to the required section profile were traditionally used as a training aid in large private gardens. These are quite easy to make up for any situation and are set over the young developing hedge row with taut lines attached to the frame structures and run along the length of the hedge or screen. Whatever means is used to develop a set profile it is desirable to keep the base width narrow from the outset.

To maintain a good shape and attractive neat appearance formal hedges and screens must be trimmed frequently, the task becoming more demanding from the third season after planting according to the natural rate of establishment.

In the case of conifers, leader shoots are best left untrimmed until the required height is reached, and for all others there should be no more than light tipping of the leaders during this period. After year one, side shoots of all subjects must be cut more severely, always with the aim during the formative years of working towards the required overall shape. It will sometimes be necessary to prune or even tie down individual shoots to ensure a good basic structure, especially near ground level.

The more trimmings carried out during a season the quicker will be the overall screen effect, and the more attractive its appearance, besides which it is much easier to maintain satisfactory shape in this way. Trimming stimulates the growth of shoots either at the point of cutting or from buds below it. The skill is to trim off relatively soft growths fractionally beyond the basic structure of the hedge or screen; and with conifers it is most important to do no more than this.

Lonicera nitida, hawthorn, blackthorn and privet especially benefit from multiple trimming to maintain good, solid shape and form and, where time can be given, trimmings in late spring, mid summer and autumn are well worthwhile. Escallonia, conifers, holly and beech are amongst the majority of subjects where shape and appearance are improved by two trimmings, made in mid summer and in mid autumn. Beech and hornbeam trimmed once in late summer will retain their desiccated leaves well into the winter in most situations. Elaeagnus and the laurels are amongst a small group which should anyway be trimmed only once per season, in the autumn – and this is the best time for the majority of species where it is only reasonably possible to trim once a year.

The effort put into careful and regular trimming of a formal hedge or screen will certainly be repaid in the production of an effective barrier and a striking garden feature attractive for its architectural line and matt or glossy finish.

INFORMAL TRAINING

Informal hedges and screens are less used in gardens than they might be. They have the advantage of needing hardly any initial training and much less effort in trimming. With less restricted plant habit there is the bonus of free flowering and fruiting, and undamaged shoots and leaf form. Once established, trimming or pruning is carried out no more than once a year. The operation

28

A fine specimen of an 8 ft (2.4 m) high hedge of Leyland cypress
(× Cupressocyparis leylandii) obtained by thoughtful early training and regular
clipping

calls for an understanding of the growth habit of the species chosen
and careful thought in carrying out the work. In the case of
flowering and fruiting plants, and those with special
characteristics such as coloured stems, the purpose is to ensure a
replenishment of young growth and removal of old, dead or
damaged wood, whilst at the same time ensuring that the main
purpose or benefit of the planting is not lost.

The range of plants for informal hedges and screens is very wide
indeed so that annual pruning needs vary, but some general
summary guidance is possible. Evergreens and species which
flower on spurs and side shoots, including camellias,
rhododendrons and pyracantha, are best not pruned regularly
beyond the removal of dead flower heads. Where there is a need to

thin congested growth to stimulate replacement shoots this is best done sparingly after flowering. Plants which flower on shoots produced in the current season, or where coloured stems are a particular feature, such as roses, fuchsias and *Cornus stolonifera*, should be pruned hard in the spring. It follows that this group is not suitable for situations where a screen is required the year round. The third group to be identified are plants which flower on wood produced in the previous season, such as escallonias, mock orange (*Philadelphus* spp.) and berberis. Necessary thinning by pruning should be selectively carried out soon after flowering time so that the plant may replenish growth in time to bear flowers in the following season.

Good pruning practice is governed by other factors such as fruit production or the ornamental value of spent flowers and seed heads. The important rule is to know as much as possible about the plant one is dealing with before planting, and this comes through experience, visiting gardens and reading.

Dwarf shrubby edging of box and lavender planted along paths or borders must be trimmed regularly for containment because they are really particularly unsightly where neglected. Two trimmings per year should be carried out on evergreen subjects, in mid summer and early autumn, and on flowering edging once, in early spring or after the flowers have withered.

CUTTING TOOLS

For the best finish to formal hedges and screens cutting tools should be chosen with thought, and the trimming work undertaken methodically and unrushed. The choice between using hand shears or a powered hedge cutter is most dependent on the scale of operation, and of course available investment. Hand shearing is certainly more time consuming but carefully done it ensures a good standard and close control of shaping. Powered hedge cutters are always more expensive and inherently more hazardous to use. Although the work can be covered more quickly than by hand shearing, hedge cutters are relatively more fatiguing to use by reason of weight, noise and concentration. Where the length of planting is modest, hand shearing is a perfectly acceptable method, but where trimming goes beyond a pleasurable or time-affordable pastime a powered hedge cutter is called for.

Choose hand shears which feel well balanced and not too heavy. It is a personal judgment, but generally quality tools at the higher end of the price range will best suit the requirement and are likely to be more easily maintained. There is no overall advantage in

The top of an overgrown hedge of yew (*Taxus baccata*) being trimmed back hard to a string marker

choosing very long-bladed shears for hedge trimming; models with a formed notch near the axis are useful for cutting out the odd thicker shoot encountered.

Mechanical hedge trimmers are powered either by petrol or electricity through mains-connected cable or built-in rechargeable battery. Petrol engine models are heavier than others and more noisy and demanding in maintenance. Electric models with a cable attachment obviously have limited range and the trailing line is often inconvenient and always potentially dangerous through severing or entanglement. Battery models are lightweight and manoeuvrable and although of rather less rapid and robust work capacity they are a good choice for the small or medium-sized garden.

It is important to read and follow all safety precautions recommended for the use of powered tools. Mains electric hedge cutters must be fitted with a circuit-breaking device, and should never be used in wet conditions. Eye protectors are advisable for use in any method of hedge and screen trimming.

Overreaching or other uncomfortable working conditions during

When using a powered trimmer it is important to keep the blade parallel to the side of the hedge

trimming are both fatiguing and dangerous. Strong, lightweight ladders should be used for tall hedges or screens, and for very substantial jobs some form of trestle and plank platform will be necessary. Always ensure that whatever is used to gain height is firmly erected, and adopt a comfortable stance during trimming work.

Trimming with hand shears should be done with a rhythmic motion. For most gardeners it will be possible to judge the straightness of the top and sides by eye, but for some it is helpful to work to a continuous line of thick cord or string fixed along the length of the hedge or screen.

It does not matter whether trimming is started at the top or bottom, but it is perhaps easier to start from the bottom where it is more convenient to work and one can stand back to assess how the straight line and finish is being developed. It helps to trim back carefully small areas along the hedge or screen as reference points which are worked towards as trimming progresses. As far as

A string marker can be used to help achieve a flat surface

possible the blades of hand shears should always be kept parallel to the required surface.

Where using a powered hedge cutter it is important to adopt a smooth and regular action with wide sweeping cuts, ensuring that the entire length of the cutter bar is engaged in the action.

For cutting informal hedges the basic tools are secateurs and long-handled pruners or loppers, with occasional recourse to a pruning saw. Here again investment in quality tools is worthwhile. Keeping shears, cutters, secateurs and saws clean, oiled and regularly sharpened or given other appropriate maintenance is an important aid to efficient and least-taxing use.

RENOVATING

It often happens that an acquired mature garden comes complete with neglected boundary hedges or screens. They may take all sorts of awful forms: gaps, bare bases and dead branches, excessive

An old hedge of *Escallonia macrantha* undergoing width reduction by drastic cutting back in early spring

height and spread, straggliness, and perhaps also choked with brambles, nettles and other perennial weeds.

Where the problem arises in long-established plantings, a judgement will have to be made as to whether the line is actually recoverable. If it is not – and that will be the more unlikely situation – the next consideration is whether or not there is space and opportunity to plant a new hedge alongside the old, either to supplement it when reasonably tidied, or replace it when in due course it is cut down to ground level or removed altogether. Where space is limited the neglected hedge or screen can be grubbed out and replanted in the same position – but this is the less acceptable option. A serious disadvantage of total grubbing out before a replanting is established is the loss of wind protection, of special importance to gardens on exposed sites.

Hedge removal is a laborious task and expensive where contracted out. There is bound to be major disturbance of the soil and the original planting line will remain prominently marked across the ground despite best efforts at restoration. Renovation of neglected hedges and screens is in most cases the best approach, and worth attempting even if more drastic action and replanting eventually proves necessary. Most woody species used for hedge and screen making respond quite satisfactorily to very severe cutting. Exactly how the renovation is tackled depends on the extent of the overgrowth. If the work is done in winter there is the advantage of absence of leaves on deciduous plants which helps in assessing progress, and there will be less disturbance to bird life. Where the planting consists predominantly of evergreens it is better to undertake renovation in April as early growth commences.

The first task is to clear out or at least pare back weed-plant invasion so that it is possible to redefine the proper width dimensions, and allow better pruning access into the bottom of the hedge or screen.

For taking overgrown plants under control one will most likely need long-arm pruners and a sharp curved pruning saw. A sharp billhook or slasher is useful, and a stout pair of gloves essential.

Leave the top of the barrier till last, concentrating on the sides and first cutting out growths which are well out of line. The main aim of side and internal thinning is to restore the hedge or screen line to reasonable bounds and to reduce the density of the barrier, thereby restoring good structure and encouraging new growth. A very general guide to the extent of thinning is to work towards a density where it is just possible to make out a helper standing on the opposite side.

Dead wood is the prime target followed by congested old branches which have proliferated from the stool. Where a hedge or screen is in active growth and, as with most deciduous subjects of a kind that will readily produce new basal shoots, the wood may be cut back to ground level if the contribution to privacy, security and shelter can be forgone. With moribund hedges or evergreen kinds it is best to restrict such hard cutting down to what is really essential removal, and to more selectively thin congested branches back to no lower than mid height. A reasonable objective is to retain hedge height but reduce the width by selective thinning.

It is very important to recognise species which can be cut back hard into old wood and those which cannot. Escallonias, hazel, hawthorn, and beech are regularly encountered examples of hedge and screen plants that will tolerate very hard cutting during renovation. Olearias, holly, lavender, broom and the majority of conifers are examples of plants which will not regenerate if treated in this way.

A common consequence of neglect is the loss of leaf and shoot growth at the base of a hedge or screen. This will usually have little effect on the sheltering function but it may be severe enough to allow intrusion, and is nearly always unsightly. It may be possible to lay down or tie in a few retained thinner shoots, and supplementary planting at the base with privet or hawthorn is cheap enough to try, though because of the inevitably poor soil structure and root competition establishment is bound to be difficult: success will depend on special care and attention to preparation of planting holes and thorough mulching. If the height of bare stems after renovation is not too great a visually acceptable and effective repair solution is the fitting of a continuous low fence of black polypropylene strapping or netting along the hedge or screen line.

Until an overgrown hedge or screen is brought fully under control and into abundant fresh growth it is difficult to establish a definite shaped profile, but a start can be made by shortening the retained branches in the middle of the barrier to the new required height and reducing the height of the others successively towards the sides. Care is needed to keep the new hedge line straight and to ensure that the finished profile is wider at the bottom than at the top. A fixed taut line, as suggested for use in regular trimming, will be helpful. Special attention must be paid to gaps in neglected plantings due to death by overcrowding and shading or wind damage. Clean out any plant remains and carefully prepare planting holes for fast-growing species, closely spaced for quick repair. All of the steps advised for establishment should be followed and because of competition from neighbouring tall survivors watering, mulching and wind protection are important.

Although it is unnecessary to give manure and fertilizer dressings to established hedges and screens which are continuously well maintained, there is a case for the supplementary feeding of renovated ones. A spring dressing of Growmore at 4 oz per sq yd (136 g per sq m) will encourage new growth, and a deep-layered mulch of organic matter applied after heavy rain is worthwhile.

Hedges and screens are valuable and expensive assets in the garden and need regular attention in order to maintain them in good condition. Although renovation is quite possible, the loss of amenity and effort required for reclamation is a high penalty to pay for neglect.

A simple post-and-string template facilitates realignment of this overgrown hedge of holly (*Ilex aquifolium*)

Suitable Plants

Almost any woody plant can be used for hedge making; and for establishing or supplementing a screen the possibilities extend to many non-woody species. Choice is dependent first on purpose and then on growing conditions, and also of course on what the gardener likes. This section describes a selection of species most tried and tested and commonly grown as formal and informal barriers. For many of them improved cultivars are available, and it is well worthwhile getting to know recommended and other possible species and cultivars through gardens, nurseries, garden centres, books and catalogues.

Many of the plants which follow are suitable for more than one purpose. Not all have common names, so these are always given secondarily in the listings. Thought should be given to the possible toxicity of plants chosen for hedges and screens which adjoin farmland or are readily accessible to children. Of the species referred to those presenting the highest potential hazard are marked as follows:

> * Some risk of poisoning to livestock consuming the foliage, especially clippings.
> † Some risk of poisoning to children attracted to berries or seed pods.

SPECIES SUITABLE FOR FORMAL OR CONTAINED HEDGES AND SCREENS

Evergreen species

Aucuba japonica A handsome shrub, with large, thick leaves which may be blotched, speckled or variegated. Suitable for sunny or shady positions. Must be trimmed to shape with secateurs.

Berberis × stenophylla Robust and spiny, with small dark green leaves. Produces long arching branches covered with golden flowers in spring. May be trimmed hard but is best treated as a semi-formal hedge.

Rhododendron ponticum is often seen as a free-growing hedge or screen in very large gardens on acid soil

Buxus sempervirens* Common box. Naturally a large shrub or small tree, but very amenable to containment by hard summer trimming of the abundant small leaves. Many garden forms including variegated ones. Suitable for medium-sized or very dwarf hedging. (See p. 13.)

Chamaecyparis lawsoniana* Lawson cypress. Makes a very good hedge or screen on a wide range of soils and sites. Numerous cultivars with green, yellow and blue-grey foliage. Best trimmed lightly in late summer.

Cotoneaster lacteus Produces large, tough leaves; the persistent large clusters of small red berries can be enjoyed following light winter trimming.

× **Cupressocyparis leylandii*** Leyland cypress. A bigeneric hybrid of great vigour, which makes a tall hedge or screen very quickly, and tolerates hard trimming. An excellent choice close planted on sites away from extreme salt-wind exposure, and where kept regularly trimmed. The foliage density and demanding roots can be problematic in a small garden. (See pp. 29 and 41.)

Cupressus macrocarpa* Monterey cypress. Fast growing, and named cultivars, especially 'Lutea', are the most reliable choice. Susceptible to cold damage as young plants, and on some sites prone to individual specimen loss in established lines. Best trimmed in late summer.

Elaeagnus macrophylla Broad leafed and robust in windy situations. A good choice for a medium-sized hedge. Does especially well in mild climate localities, and produces small sweetly scented flowers in autumn. E. × ebbingei is closely related, and faster growing. Best trimmed in mid summer.

Escallonia macrantha Not reliably hardy inland but very quickly makes an excellent strong hedge in maritime areas where it is most tolerant of salt-laden winds. 'Crimson Spire' and 'Red Hedger' are attractive; E. 'Langleyensis' and the 'Donard' cultivars are hardier and suitable for formal training. (See p. 34.)

Euonymus japonicus† Thrives in sun or shade and is much planted near the sea and in towns. The small glossy green leaves are attractive, but on some sites become disfigured with mildew infection in summer.

Garrya elliptica Makes an effective semi-formal hedge where lightly pruned with secateurs in the spring. On the widely available

The golden-foliaged Leyland cypress, × Cupressocyparis leylandii 'Castlewellan'

male form of the plant the attractiveness of the bluish green leaves is enhanced by striking grey catkins produced during winter months. *Griselinia littoralis* A good choice for relatively frost-free areas, especially close to the sea. Naturally a tall-growing shrub, the plant responds well to the trimming of its strong, bright green leaves which are borne on yellow stems. (See p. 42.)

Ilex aquifolium† Common holly. A versatile plant useful for a protective barrier, also for its attractive tough foliage which withstands exposure to strong wind, and salt and pollutant-laden atmosphere. Rather slow growing. *I.* × *altaclerensis* includes many excellent hybrids with larger leaves, and all are very suitable for making tall screens or hedges. Holly hedges should be carefully trimmed in the formative years to ensure that shoots are furnished to ground level. When well established, regular trimming is tolerated and best done in late summer. (See pp. 37 and 42.)

Ligustrum ovalifolium*† Oval-leafed privet. The commonest of all garden hedge plants, usually evergreen but may lose its leaves in cold districts and near to the sea. The green foliage is prolific and requires trimming several times each season. Root activity is competitive which can be a marked disadvantage in small gardens. Yellow and variegated-leafed cultivars available. (See p. 44.)

Lonicera nitida A plant of dense habit with small leaves borne on tough shoots. Fast growing and must be hard trimmed several times each season, and carefully shaped to overcome its tendency to fall apart especially under the weight of snow. More attractive is 'Baggesen's Gold', with predominantly yellow leaves. (See pp. 26 and 45.)

Olearia macrodonta New Zealand holly. A bold hedging plant for coastal gardens, bearing holly-like leaves on strong, flaky stems. Bears fragrant white daisy-like flowers in early summer. Best trimmed lightly in mid summer after flowering. *O. solandri* and *O. traversii* are other possibilities for coastal areas. (See p. 46.)

Osmanthus delavayi Slow growing but worthy of patience for its excellent small glossy leaves and abundant, fragrant white flowers produced in early summer. Quite adaptable, and should be lightly trimmed in mid summer.

Pittosporum tenuifolium Reliably hardy only in maritime areas for which it is a good choice. Attractive small, glossy, bright-green,

Above: Holly forms a prickly barrier for boundaries. Shown here is *Ilex aquifolium* 'Silver Queen'

Below: Glossy-leafed *Griselinia littoralis* is particularly well suited to seaside locations

Above: *Ligustrum ovalifolium* 'Argenteum' is an attractive form of the adaptable oval-leafed privet

Opposite: A well-contained hedge of the yellow foliage form of *Lonicera nitida*, 'Baggesen's Gold'

undulate leaves, borne on dark stems. Can be trimmed in spring or autumn. There are a number of cultivars with attractive leaf colour and markings. *P. crassifolium* has larger, tougher leaves, is much faster growing and has a wider hardiness range.

Prunus laurocerasus* Common laurel. Widely tolerant and fast growing, with large glossy leaves. Vigour and density make it an excellent choice for a semi-formal hedge or screen. For containment it should only be lightly trimmed with secateurs in spring.

Quercus ilex Evergreen oak. Slow growing but very suitable as a trimmed hedge. Leaves are leathery and dark green; the oldest are shed in spring and may be a nuisance in a small garden. Stands well in exposure except in the coldest inland areas.

Taxus baccata*† English yew. One of the best choices for hedges and screens, especially well suited to larger gardens. Tolerant of a wide range of conditions and amenable to shaping and hard trimming, which is best done in late summer. (See pp. 4, 10, 24 and 31.)

Thuja plicata* Western red cedar. Its vigorous bright green glossy growth quickly produces a hedge or screen. Tolerates trimming well, which is best done in late summer so that subsequent shoot growth is sufficiently hardened to withstand frost.

Olearia macrodonta is a good choice for a robust and attractive hedge in seaside gardens

Deciduous species
Alnus glutinosa Common alder. Suitable as a tall, narrow hedge or screen especially on wet sites. The young growth and catkins produced in spring are attractive. *Alnus cordata*, Italian alder, is faster growing and a most elegant tree, which should be considered for large gardens. (See p. 20.)

Carpinus betulus Hornbeam. Excellent and easily grown. Generally similar in trained habit to beech, but more cold-tolerant and distinguished particularly by its saw-toothed leaf margins, rougher texture, and characteristic bracted fruit clusters. If trimmed in late summer a large proportion of the crisp, dead leaves are retained until spring. (See pp. 23 and 47.)

Corylus avellana Hazel. Its multi-stemmed habit makes for a well-furnished, strong hedge and screen plant adaptable to most situations. Yellow autumn leaf colour is a bonus, as are the yellow catkins of spring where the plants are lightly trimmed.

Crataegus monogyna May or common hawthorn. A valuable boundary hedge plant with deterring thorns. Suitable as a short or tall hedge or screen; the mass of white flowers in spring is spectacular. Stands up well to hard trimming which is best done in mid summer, although tolerates cutting at any time.

Hornbeam (*Carpinus betulus*) establishes easily as a hedge and responds well to trimming

Fagus sylvatica Common beech. Thrives on all well-drained sites to make an excellent hedge or screen. Prized for its wind hardiness, attractive appearance and tolerance of hard trimming. Bright green, smooth leaves turn copper yellow in autumn. Where trimmed in late August the dead brown foliage will last until spring. For low-lying sites where the new season's growth may be damaged by frost, hornbeam is a better choice (qv). Purple-leafed beech are available from seedling selections, or as the best dark-leafed clone F. 'Riversii' which being vegetatively propagated is more expensive. (See p. 16.)

Hippophaë rhamnoides Sea buckthorn. Very tolerant of salt-laden winds and suitable for the outer defence of coastal gardens; also succeeds inland. Attractive silvery willow-like leaves, and orange berries borne on male plants. Best lightly trimmed to shape in late summer.

Populus spp. Poplar. Very vigorous, especially on wet sites, and suitable for windbreak and screen planting on the boundaries of very large gardens. Roots can invade drains and, particularly on clay soils, may damage building foundations. P. alba, white poplar, succeeds on coastal sites; P. nigra 'Plantierensis' is similar to the Lombardy poplar but preferable to it. Hybrids of P. balsamifera and P. trichocarpa, for example 'Balsam Spire' ("TT 32") have proved very satisfactory for large sites.

Prunus cerasifera Myrobalan. Fast growing, making a strong, dense hedge which tolerates hard trimming. Very suitable for exposed or coastal sites, and there are a number of purple-leafed cultivars. P. spinosa, blackthorn, is a thorny relative with dark branches, a good alternative to hawthorn as an excluding barrier. Both are best pruned in summer although tolerant of cutting at any time.

Salix spp. Willow. Fast growing and does well on wet sites. As with poplars the roots can invade drains and foundations so that special thought must be given before planting in small gardens. S. alba, white willow, is an elegant species which does well also near to the sea. S. caprea, the native goat willow, can be contained as a moderate-sized hedge and bears attractive catkins in spring. S. daphnoides and S. purpurea and their cultivars have attractive purple shoots. Willows are suitable for running up as screens and for this purpose can be pruned occasionally or pollarded at height. They may also be trained semi-formally as hedge plants by regular light trimming in late summer, or by stooling to ground level in spring where the coloured shoots are prized as a garden feature and continuous shelter is not important.

The tamarisks (*Tamarix pentandra* and *T. tetrandra*) make good spreading hedges and screens in seaside locations, and their soft pink flowers are attractive

Sambucus nigra† Elder. A native plant undistinguished for garden use, but very suitable as a windbreak hedge on account of its rugged nature. Amenable to containment by hard trimming, best done with secateurs in the spring and again in late summer. There are a number of cultivars with variegated or interestingly shaped leaves.

Sorbus intermedia Swedish whitebeam. Makes a robust, narrow-leafed hedge or screen on account of its upright stems. Equally suited to urban, rural and maritime sites; should be close planted, and trimmed in late summer. *S. aria*, the native whitebeam, can be used and there are some interesting cultivars, notably 'Lutescens'.

Symphoricarpos albus† Snowberry. An effective hedge on a wide range of garden sites; attractive for its slender foliage and pink flowers in spring followed by white berries. Unsuitable as an exposed boundary hedge. Trim in winter to enjoy the effect of its berries.

Tamarix pentandra Tamarisk. A versatile plant which stands well in exposure very close to the sea. Tolerant of trimming to a contained shape, best done in late summer to avoid the hedge becoming straggly and bare. Flowers from mid summer, whereas *T. tetrandra* which is equally suitable flowers in the spring and should be trimmed soon afterwards.

SPECIES SUITABLE FOR INFORMAL HEDGES AND SCREENS

Evergreen species

Arbutus unedo Strawberry tree. A small ericaceous tree tolerant of alkaline soils and exposure to wind. Does particularly well in maritime areas, producing small, strawberry-like fruits in autumn. Mature specimens have attractive rich brown shredded bark. Trim sparingly after autumn flowering and fruiting.

Atriplex halimus Tree purslane. Survives well in windy situations, including coastal sites where it can produce a hedge up to 6 ft (1.8 m) in height. Silvery grey foliage. Light trimming of damaged shoots should be done in early spring.

Berberis buxifolia A spiny hedge subject up to $3\frac{1}{4}$ ft (1 m) high with box-like leaves. Slow growing, producing dark purple fruits. Where necessary, light trimming should be done in early spring. *B. darwinii* is an excellent flowering shrub with attractive small, holly-like leaves. Will make a hedge up to 8 ft (2.4 m) where well grown. Produces sprays of orange flowers in spring, after which any necessary trimming should be done.

Brachyglottis 'Sunshine' Formerly known as *Senecio* 'Sunshine', this grows up to $3\frac{1}{4}$ ft (1 m) high bearing a profusion of daisy-like flowers and tough grey foliage, making it an excellent choice in exposed or maritime areas. *B. monroi* is of similar habit with wavy leaf margins. Both respond to pruning, which is necessary to

Brachyglottis 'Sunshine' is at its most attractive where allowed to grow freely and can be trimmed as a low formal hedge

preserve a shapely form: best done in late autumn to allow benefit of interesting seed heads.

Camellia japonica Common camellia. Large, glossy-leafed shrub of which there are very many named free-flowering cultivars. Will grow to great height in shade or sun. The C. × *williamsii* group and others are equally suitable. Normally requires minimal trimming, beyond deadheading where the flowers are retained; occasional thinning is best done in spring after flowering.

Ceanothus thyrsiflorus A tall, vigorous hardy shrub producing clusters of pale blue flowers in early summer. The more tender C. *dentatus* and C. 'Trewithen Blue' are good choices for mild climate areas. Where necessary, light trimming should be done immediately after flowering.

Choisya ternata Mexican orange blossom. Does well over a wide range of situations, although the glossy foliage suffers in exposure. Can reach a height of 8 ft (2.4 m). The white flowers of early spring and summer are sweetly scented. Minimal trimming advisable.

Cotoneaster franchetii Good internal hedge and screen plant up to about 10 ft (3 m) in height. Shoots of dark green leaves bear scarlet berries. C. 'Cornubia' is a suitable choice for a screen up to at least 15 ft (4.5 m) in height and is abundant with berries. C. *microphyllus* makes a low, spreading hedge. Where necessary, light pruning should be done in late summer.

Cotoneaster franchetii sternianus is one of a group of plants providing the added interest of berries to an informal hedge

Escallonia **'Apple Blossom'** This attractively pink and white flowered cultivar is representative of many evergreen escallonias which make excellent informal hedges up to 8 ft (2.4 m) high. They benefit from some annual shoot thinning in late summer.

Hebe salicifolia A suitable choice for a hedge up to 6 ft (1.8 m) in height in mild climate areas. Bears long, pointed leaves and white or mauve flowers in mid summer. Many other suitable species and cultivars of which *H.* 'Autumn Glory' makes an attractive dwarf hedge. Occasional light pruning is best done in spring.

Lavandula angustifolia Lavender. Succeeds on a wide range of sites and soils, making an excellent border edging up to $3\frac{1}{4}$ ft (1 m) high. Popular for its aromatic blue flower spikes borne in profusion in mid summer on rounded plants of grey-green foliage. Notable cultivars are *L.* 'Hidcote', *L.* 'Munstead' and *L.* 'Loddon Pink'. Should be close clipped below the flowering spikes in early spring to avoid a straggly habit. To maintain vigour and quality of growth and flower, plan for replacement within 10 years. (See p. 13.)

Mahonia aquifolium **hybrids** Oregon grape. Suited for a hedge of up to 5 ft (1.5 m) in height. The glossy green leaves turn bronze and red in winter, and bright yellow flowers of spring produce blue-black berries. A good choice for shady situations. Where necessary, light pruning is best done in late winter.

Pseudosasa japonica Bamboo. Hardy, vigorous and wind tolerant. Does particularly well in mild, wet districts. Provides a decorative, dense hedge or screen up to 8 ft (2.4 m) in height but the roots are invasive. *Sinarundinaria nitida* is an elegant species of bamboo with smaller leaves.

Pyracantha coccinea Firethorn. An interesting hedge and screen subject, up to 8 ft (2.4 m) high, which succeeds under a wide range of conditions including wind exposure. The hybrids are most suitable. Formidable spines make it a good choice for a secure barrier. The hawthorn-like flowers of summer are followed by clusters of red berries. Where necessary prune lightly in spring.

Rhododendron ponticum* Widely planted. A vigorous shrub which grows up to 20 ft (6 m) on non-chalky soils to form a robust hedge or screen. Tolerant of shade. Produces mauve flowers in early summer. Minimal pruning required, beyond deadheading where the flowers are retained. Occasional thinning best done after flowering. (See p. 38.)

Many *Hebe* spp., such as *H. brachysiphon* seen here, make a good choice for a flowering hedge or screen

Rosmarinus officinalis Rosemary. Attains a hedge height of up to 6 ft (1.8 m). The tough grey-green leaves are strongly scented; numerous blue flowers produced in spring. Light pruning and shoot thinning may be done after flowering to avoid a straggly form.

Santolina chamaecyparissus Cotton lavender. An attractive grey foliage plant with bright yellow flowers suitable for a low hedge up to 2 ft (0.6 m) in height. Trim lightly after flowering.

Viburnum tinus Laurustinus. A valuable choice for its long flowering period from autumn until spring. Tolerant of exposure and a wide range of conditions except extreme cold. Dense, glossy foliage which where necessary should be pruned in spring.

Deciduous species

Amelanchier lamarckii Forms a variously interesting upright hedge or screen to at least 15 ft (4.5 m). Bronze-tinged emerging growths are attractive, with foliage turning from green to copper red in autumn. Clusters of white flowers are borne in early summer, followed by green berries which ripen to very dark red. Minimal pruning as necessary in spring.

Chaenomeles speciosa Suitable for a medium-sized hedge, to 5 ft (1.5 m) which produces beautiful bright red flowers in spring. Many cultivars with crimson, pink and double flowers; also dwarf forms. Prune straggly shoots especially, after flowering.

Cornus stolonifera A strong-growing plant, valued for its dark red stems, which is suitable for an inner hedge up to 8 ft (2.4 m) high. The cultivar 'Flaviramea' produces yellow stems. Both make striking garden features in autumn and winter, and the stem colour is most intense on young wood. Best hard pruned in spring.

Cytisus scoparius Common broom. Representative of many brooms suitable for a medium-sized hedge. Bears bright yellow pea-like flowers and small leaves on long stems. Many cultivars with flower colour ranging from white to crimson. Prune selectively after flowering, near to the base of current shoots and never into old wood.

Deutzia scabra An upright-branched, easily grown shrub which makes a hedge or screen to about 8 ft (2.4 m) high. White flowers are borne in mid summer. There are cultivars with double and variously red-shaded flowers. Prune selectively after flowering.

Forsythia × intermedia A sturdy-growing hybrid suitable for an internal hedge up to 10 ft (3 m) high. Produces bright yellow flowers in early spring. Prune hard after flowering.

Fuchsia magellanica An elegant, free-flowering plant, bearing

Fuchsia magellanica 'Variegata' provides flower and foliage interest as a hedge

graceful pendulous flowers in spring. At its best in mild climate areas, but regenerates in inland areas where sometimes cut down by frost. Best pruned hard in spring.

Hydrangea macrophylla* Representative of a large group of shrubs which are easily grown as hedge plants provided the soil is moisture retentive. Numerous cultivars which may be divided into the Hortensias or mop-heads and Lacecaps, and these most usually grow to 6 ft (1.8 m) in height. Best pruned by deadheading and reducing the number of flowered shoots in late autumn.

Hypericum forrestii* Like *H. beanii* and *H. pseudohenryi*, with which there is some confusion in nurseries, this plant has value as a medium-height hedge, generally up to 5 ft (1.5 m). Abundant large, bright yellow flowers of mid summer are attractive. Best hard pruned in spring.

Kerria japonica Useful for hedge-making up to 6 ft (1.8 m) high, and valued for its bright green stems in winter. Produces yellow flowers in spring and early summer. There are double flowers and variegated leaf forms. Best pruned after flowering; needs containment on account of its suckering.

Rosa hugonis for flower interest

Perovskia atriplicifolia Forms an elegant feature hedge up to 4 ft
(1.2 m) high. Bears aromatic narrow leaves on grey stems; useful for
its blue flowers of late summer. Best hard pruned in spring.
Philadelphus coronarius Mock orange. Strong growing to form a
hedge or screen up to 10 ft (3 m) high. Has a mass of small, off-white
sweetly-scented flowers in mid summer. Many other species and
cultivars of this genus are suitable as informal hedges and screens.
Prune flower stems as the blooms fade.
Ribes sanguineum Flowering currant. Of strong habit, suitable for
a hedge up to 8 ft (2.4 m) high. Very attractive in early spring when it
produces conspicuous trusses of pink flowers. R. 'King Edward
VII' is an improved cultivar bearing large crimson flowers.
Flowered stems should be pruned as the blooms fade.

Rosa moyesii especially for fruit interest

Rosa spp. Most of the rose species and bush hybrids are suitable for hedge-making. Range of flower size, presentation and colour is wide; also leaf, stem and fruit form. R. *hugonis* and R. *moyesii* are two species particularly worth considering. (See p. 62.)
Spiraea × arguta Makes a hedge up to 6 ft (1.8 m) high. Clusters of small, pure white flowers borne on arching branches in late spring. Representative of many spiraeas suitable for an informal hedge. S. 'Anthony Waterer' makes a dwarf hedge, up to 4 ft (1.2 m) high, with flat-headed clusters of crimson flowers in mid summer. Best pruned after flowering.
Weigela florida Grows to at least 8 ft (2.4 m) high, and bears funnel-shaped red flowers in mid summer. Wide choice of hybrids. Prune flowered stems after blooms fade.

Artificial Screens and Fences

Reference to screens has so far been in the context of rows of living plants grown specifically for protection and to mask unsightly views and objects. Establishment and maintenance considerations for such features are almost always the same as those for hedges. It is however quite possible to obtain most of the benefits of screening in the garden by using structures and fences made of rigid fabricated materials.

A primary advantage over plant forms is the provision of immediate screening and shelter. For wind shelter purpose the structures can be manufactured to near the theoretically ideal permeability ratio of 60% solid : 40% porosity, and where carefully fixed and maintained this remains constant. Where wind shelter is essential solid screens and fences should not be chosen, for reasons previously discussed. However, where they already exist or are otherwise a necessity the potentially damaging production of air turbulence to leeward can be reduced by thick plantings of shrubby species allowed to grow up above the screen height. The same consideration applies to stone wall boundaries which can often be top layered with turves or soil upon which scrubby plants such as gorse (Ulex spp.) can be planted with the object of filtering the wind.

It is unnecessary for the cladding of fabricated screens and fences constructed primarily for wind shelter to be extended to ground level. A gap of up to one fifth of the total height of the barrier is generally acceptable and will afford cost economy; but of course this option must take account of the degree of exposure and sensitivity of the plants to be protected.

With certain types of non-living screens and fences there is the advantage of ready movability, and they are a valuable means of nursing a young hedge, shelter belt and other kinds of plantings in the early years.

Above: A wood panel screen made more visually attractive and put to productive use by the planting of an espalier pear

Below: A durable low-level screen of extruded plastic net

Non-living screens and fences often make attractive garden features, especially where plant associations are planned. They can be valuable in giving height and interest and opportunity for the cultivation of climbing plants. Where panel-type fences are encountered or chosen to surround boundaries it is almost always desirable to mask their conspicuous appearance by growing attractive plants in front or trained upon them.

Manufactured screens and fences take up minimal space and do not present all of the competitive effects on cropping experienced with living barriers. In most cases, however, this type of garden feature is likely to be more expensive in capital outlay than plant hedges and screens.

There is wide choice of form and materials for non-living screens and fences. They can be made of patterned hollow concrete blocks in a variety of shapes, colours and finishes. These structures should be restricted to more formal areas, especially near to the house, for extravagantly handled elsewhere in the plan they can destroy the natural ambience sought in garden design by most people. Neutral colours for concrete screens are easiest to live with.

More widespread is the use of wood for screens and fences. Softwoods treated with brown preservative are the best choice; painted wood requires more regular maintenance but has a place in formal areas.

Occasionally, wire netting offers a suitable barrier and cladding where a scrambling species is planted to cover it. More often the preferred cladding will be fabricated plastic in either woven or extruded forms, and there are many types and qualities available to choose from. The commonest colour range is green, off-white, brown and black, and though there are bound to be individual preferences, in the interests of sympathetic appearance in the garden one would do well to consider black first and green last.

Tall cladded screens of over 5 ft (1.5 m) height need to be permanently fixed with substantial supports. These are an expensive choice suited to situations where the establishment of tall plants is not practicable because of land availability or on an extremely exposed coastal site; or perhaps where it is necessary to screen an undesirable view immediately. Suitable proprietary cladding materials are plastic strapping and extruded or woven polypropylene and all must be of heavy gauge for this purpose. For economy and improved visual effect tall screens may be formed by cladding only the top half of the structure and infilling the lower part with a shrubby species, trimmed or allowed to grow informally depending on location.

A medium-height screen of a proprietary heavy-duty plastic strapping

Structures of less than 5 ft (1.5 m) height are suitable for short-term screening, and can be made of either portable rigid sections or removable fabric. They are particularly useful for nursing young hedge plants, or as movable wind protection within a large expanse of garden where a permanent hedge or screen is not appropriate. Wooden screens 4 ft (1:2 m) high in 10 ft (3 m) lengths are widely used, the framework clad with 1 in. (2.5 cm) wide vertical wooden laths spaced 1 in. (2.5 cm) apart. Less expensive for a continuous low screen are plastic nettings which come in a variety of forms and grades.

Angle iron stakes are very suitable for supporting the low, ready-made, portable wooden screens described, to which they are fixed with wire ties. For flexible sorts of cladding to any height, round wooden post supports are stronger and cheaper than square ones and they should be peeled and preserved for durability. Secure anchorage depends upon the diameter of support posts used and their embedding depth; and these considerations are affected by basic wind speed and soil type, screen height and cladding

A low-level fence of posts and wire clad with scrambling roses. Such a structure is sometimes referred to as a 'fedge'

material, spacing between supports and the timber species, and whether or not concrete is used.

Technical data is available to cover all combinations but for most garden situations of moderate exposure, where a screen of more than 13 ft (4 m) height is unlikely, the following guidelines are suitable:

Screen height above ground level	Support post diameter	Support post spacing	Embedding depth
5–13 ft (1.5–4 m)	4–6 in. (100–150 mm)	Same as screen height above ground level	$\frac{1}{3}$ screen height above ground level
< 5 ft (1.5 m)	3½ in. (90 mm)	Twice screen height above ground level	$\frac{1}{4}$–$\frac{1}{3}$ screen height above ground level

A substantial nylon net screen on an exposed site, back planted on the windward side with trees for improved visual effect. Wind deflection benefits establishment

All claddings should be attached to the windward side of the support posts. Some of the heaviest grades of proprietary cladding materials come with custom-made fixings; other types will require top and bottom attachment to continuous runs of galvanised steel wire (11–8 gauge), by carefully threading polypropylene twine through and along the back-folded fabric.

The construction of tall screens requires mechanical aid, with each support post being secured by concreting, or by the attachment of pairs of anchoring wooden sleepers below ground level with the infill soil power-rammed. The ends of all artificial screens should be reinforced with buttress support posts or guy lines; and during cladding the fabric must be kept as taut as possible, which calls for care and assistance.

Index

Page numbers in **bold** refer to illustrations